NATIONAL GEOGRAPHIC

Passion for Parrots

PATHFINDER EDITION

Dr. Jamie Gilardi with Rebecca L. Johnson
and Cristina G. Mittermeier

CONTENTS

2 Parrots in Peril

7 Peek at Parrots

8 Parrot People

12 Concept Check

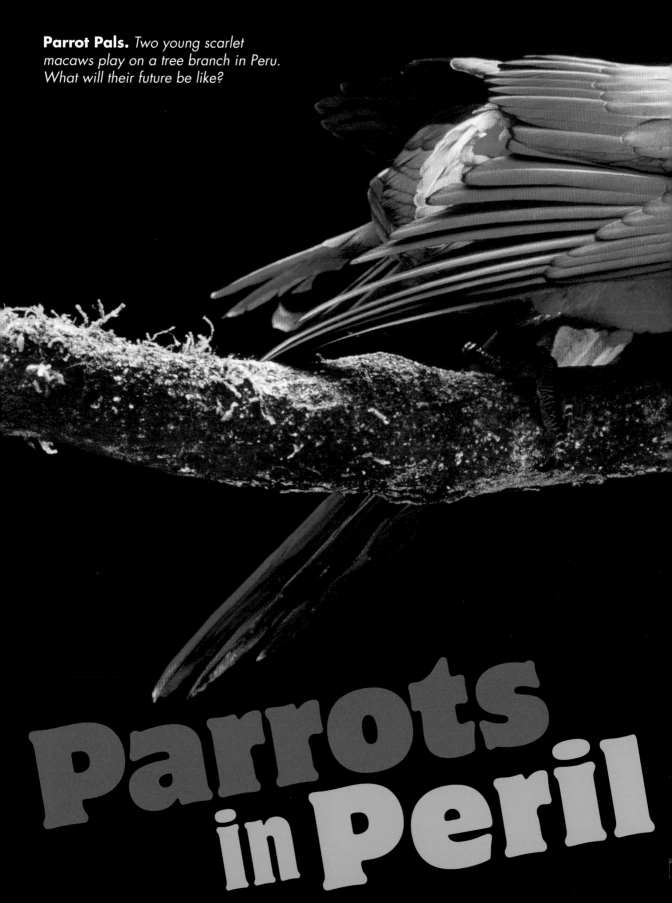

Parrot Pals. *Two young scarlet macaws play on a tree branch in Peru. What will their future be like?*

Parrots in Peril

Because parrots are beautiful and smart, people have trapped millions over the years to sell as pets. Come to Peru to see what's being done to save wild parrots.

Coffee-colored water laps gently against our canoe. It's just before dawn, and we're heading down the Urubamba River in central Peru. The river winds through the western edge of South America's vast Amazon rain forest. As the boatman guides the canoe toward shore, I shoulder my pack.

Ten minutes later, I am inside a tiny hut hidden in the trees. I look out to see a steep cliff of red-brown clay on the riverbank. The sun is just rising. I hear the clay-eaters coming!

Blue-headed parrots are first. A flock swoops in on wings of brilliant green, squawking and screeching as they scrabble for footholds on the cliff. Each bird gobbles up a thumb-sized lump of clay. Next the red-and-green and scarlet macaws arrive. Together, the birds make a rainbow of colors.

By Dr. Jamie Gilardi with Rebecca L. Johnson

3

A Mystery Solved

I'm a biologist—a scientist who studies living things. In my case, I study birds. I have come to Peru to learn more about rain forest parrots. To see the birds, I visit a clay lick on a riverbank near the village of Sepahua. This is a place where parrots eat clay. Hundreds of parrots come here every morning.

Scientists started coming to Peru's Amazon rain forest to study parrots in the 1980s. That's when they first saw the clay licks. My first trip to Peru was in the early 1990s. I wanted to find out why the parrots ate clay, so I watched the birds carefully. I collected the foods they ate and took samples of the clay they ate, too. Then I ran some tests in a lab back in the U.S.

What I found was that rain forests parrots eat a lot of seeds, and many of the seeds contain toxins, or poisonous chemicals. The toxins can be harmful if they build up in a bird's body. The clay prevents the toxins from getting into the parrots' bodies in the first place.

Beauty and Brains

I could spend hours watching parrots at a clay lick. They are some of the world's most beautiful birds, and they're never boring. Parrots are great fliers, but they are also incredible acrobats. They can climb trees, reach for fruit, and even hang upside down by a single toe!

Parrots have strong family ties, and many probably mate for life. They seem to like each other's company, too. Their screechy, squawky voices fill the forest with a symphony of chatter.

Some types of parrots are able to imitate human speech. The amazing thing is that they're not just making noise. When they speak, they are using sounds to communicate. There's no doubt—parrots are smart. They are some of the world's most intelligent animals.

Being brainy and beautiful, though, has created problems for parrots. People everywhere want them as pets. Worldwide, millions of wild parrots have been captured for the **pet trade**, and many parrot populations are at risk. It's pushed some, such as New Zealand's kakapo (kah-kuh-PO), to near extinction.

Marvelous Mudpies. *Eating clay protects these macaws from toxins and gives them needed minerals.*

Hanging Out. *Parrots have four strong toes that help them climb and reach fruit.*

Taking Action

Fortunately, conservation groups took up the challenge. They met with government officials in Peru and shared what scientists had learned. They explained that Peru's parrots could be wiped out completely. Some officials listened. Since parrots are safe inside national parks, the government expanded the parks inside the rain forest, which included several important parrot clay licks.

For the clay licks that lie outside park boundaries, conservation groups used a different strategy. They started ecotourism projects. World Parrot Trust worked closely with local communities, helping them build small lodges near some of the largest licks.

Now tourists from all over the world come to stay at these lodges. Local guides take them to see parrots. Many people from nearby villages work at the lodges, and some help manage them. The money the lodges make from tourists doesn't just go toward protecting parrots; it helps protect wildlife in thousands of acres of Peruvian rain forest.

Parrots at Risk

It took a while for parrot hunters to reach the Sepahua clay lick. The rain forest is thick in this remote part of Peru. For centuries, the only people living here were the Machiguenga Indians. They sometimes killed parrots for food, and even kept a few as pets, but their impact on the parrot population was small.

Then outsiders began arriving. Miners came in search of gold, loggers in search of trees to cut down, and trappers in search of parrots.

The trappers were not shy. They were eager to capture Peruvian parrots for the international pet trade, and parrots that gathered at clay licks were easy targets.

We scientists felt that something had to be done to protect the parrots and the clay licks. Parrot trappers take as many birds as they can, and we worried that the clay licks soon would be empty. Would the parrots' chatter end?

Nut Cracker. *This blue-and-yellow macaw uses its powerful beak to crush and eat a hard Brazil nut.*

Homemade Help. *People make and sell beautiful* arpilleras *to help protect wild parrots.*

Parrot Art

You won't find an ecotourism lodge near Sepahua, though. The village is deep in the forest and is too hard for tourists to reach. Still, the parrots at the Sepahua lick are protected. Where does the money come from to keep them safe? It comes from art.

People in Sepahua make *arpilleras* (ar-pee-YE-ras). They are beautiful cloth wall hangings that show life in the forest around the village. Look closely and you may see people, flowers, trees—and parrots, of course! Money made from selling the art pays for guards to watch over the Sepahua clay lick and another clay lick nearby.

Wordwise

More Progress for Parrots

The parrots I'm watching at Sepahua lick are safe from trappers for now, but parrots are still legally trapped for the pet trade in other parts of Peru. Scientists and conservation groups are trying to change that. The government has limited the number of parrots that trappers can take. We're hoping that this important first step will eventually lead to a ban, or stop, of all trade in wild parrots.

When it does, Peru will join countries like Indonesia and Mexico, which have stopped **exporting** parrots caught in the wild. Many countries have stopped **importing** them, too. Europeans, for example, had been importing around 2 million wild birds every year! In 2007, the European Union decided to ban that practice, which in turn ended almost all legal import and export of wild birds.

Since 1993, no parrots caught in the wild have been allowed to enter the United States, either. The parrots you see in pet shops have been raised **in captivity**. Think hard before buying one, though. A parrot needs huge amounts of attention and care, and some can live for more than 50 years.

Living Wild and Free

The future is looking brighter for wild parrots worldwide. We still have a long way to go to protect them completely, but there's been progress in many places around the world.

Some parrots are even making a comeback. In the 1980s, only a dozen or so small, green echo parakeets survived. Today, their population is more than 300 strong!

Progress in helping parrots proves what you may have heard before. People working together can make a difference.

That's why the *arpilleras* are so remarkable. In a simple, colorful way, they connect a place as remote as Sepahua with the outside world. The *arpilleras* seem to say, "See our parrots in the wild. See how beautiful they are." When you get the message, you understand why wild parrots don't belong in cages. They belong in the forest, forever flying free.

Peek at PARROTS

Y ou can hear the squawk and screech of parrots in many warm regions of the world. There are over 350 types of these brainy and beautiful birds. They all have strong, curved beaks and four toes. But that's where most of the similarities end. Take a peek at their many colors and sizes. Which parrot is your favorite?

The beautiful crown of yellow feathers on the head of this cockatoo opens like a fan when the bird is alarmed.

Flying over much of West Africa, noisy Senegal parrots chatter to each other with whistles and squawks.

As a rainbow lorikeet eats, pollen and nectar from flowers stick to tiny hairs on its tongue.

The critically endangered kakapo of New Zealand is the world's heaviest parrot and also the only flightless parrot.

rrot People

native people of the Amazon rain forest.

e surrounded by
ess. At first, I don't
where I am. Then I
er that I'm far from home
age in Brazil, a country in
merica. I have come to take
of **rain forest** people.
and wet, I cuddle into
ket and dream about the
re that awaits me.

Little Faces

A few minutes later, the sun rises, and
I see many small faces peeking at me
through my mosquito net! They belong
to the children of a rain forest people
called the Kayapó. I smile at them.

The village they live in is known as
Kendjam. Clearly, the kids want to show
me their home, so I grab my camera and
follow them.

By Cristina G. Mittermeier

Village Views

When we enter the village, I notice that it is made up of huts that stand in a circle. The roofs of the huts are made of palm fronds gathered from rain forest trees.

The Kayapó consider their rain forest home to be a very special place because they find food, water, shelter, and medicine here.

Around me I see other forest items. Leaves are laced together to make shelter and clothing, sticks are carved to make tools, and turtle shells are used as bowls.

As we walk through the village, a girl comes out of a hut. She is holding something red, white, blue, and yellow. It is a beautiful parrot known as a scarlet macaw!

Cristina Mittermeier

AREA ENLARGED SOUTH AMERICA

ATLANTIC OCEAN

Amazon River

AMAZON RAIN FOREST

•Kendjam

B R A Z I L

N W E S

Brasília ★

	Rain forest
	River
	Boundary
★	Capital
•	Village

Rain Forest River.
The Iriri River in Brazil flows near Kayapó lands.

Fabulous Feathers

The Kayapó pluck parrot feathers to make *kokai*. These are **headdresses** that the Kayapó wear at celebrations and to show their **status**. They also wear them to frighten enemies.

I see macaws hopping around the village. The Kayapó keep these partly plucked birds as pets. I watch the girl take her pet into a nearby hut. She motions me to follow her inside.

The hut is dark because there are no windows. As my eyes adjust to the darkness, I start to see shapes. On a table, I see a green macaw with bald spots where feathers have been plucked.

An old man is sitting on the floor sorting feathers. He puts the different colors into various piles. He will use the feathers to make a new headdress.

Forest Farewell

The Kayapó are a wonderful people, but I cannot spend much time with them. The next morning, I get up early to fly home. I think about the amazing things I have seen. Truly, the rain forest world of the Kayapó is magical.

WORDWISE

headdress: head covering, often with special meaning

rain forest: wooded area that gets at least ten centimeters (four inches) of rain a month

status: a person's position in a group

Praise for
PARROTS

It's time to swoop in to find out what you have learned about parrots.

1 Why do parrots eat clay? How did Dr. Gilardi figure out the answer to this question?

2 What problems do parrots still face in some parts of Peru? How are people trying to help them?

3 Are efforts to protect wild parrots working? Explain.

4 How are the many types of parrots similar? How are they different?

5 How do parrots help the Kayapó people preserve their culture?